T0355003

BREATHING
Sorrow

BREATHING Sorrow

A journey
through grief
and the pathway to
reluctant survival

CAROLE-ANN BAER

Archway Publishing books may be ordered through booksellers or by contacting:

Archway Publishing
1663 Liberty Drive
Bloomington, IN 47403
www.archwaypublishing.com
844-669-3957

ISBN: 978-1-6657-6458-2 (sc)
ISBN: 978-1-6657-6460-5 (hc)
ISBN: 978-1-6657-6459-9 (e)

Library of Congress Control Number: 2024916684

Print information available on the last page.

Archway Publishing rev. date: 10/31/2024

Now something so sad has hold of us that the breath leaves and we can't even cry.

Charles Bukowski, *"You Get So Alone at Times That It Just Makes Sense"*

CONTENTS

FOREWORD

Lee Baer was my oldest and dearest friend, and when he married Carole Ann, she became my dear friend as well. When Lee was first diagnosed with metastatic cancer, his family, friends, and I experienced a myriad of confusing emotions, including hope and fear. Carole Ann and her children, of course, suffered most of all. To understand their journey, first you have to know who Lee was, both intellectually and emotionally.

Lee was a brilliant man who, during his remarkable career as a clinical psychologist, helped many to understand obsessive-compulsive disorder, his main area of study. As he learned about the different facets of OCD, he used this knowledge to treat and have a profound and positive influence on his patients.

Lee's intellectual and scientific achievements, however, only scratch the surface of who he was as a man. He cared deeply about everyone whose life he touched. He was a dedicated, caring husband and father, and his family was his most precious achievement. He loved them deeply and unconditionally. He was also a good friend, a man who stood by me and my family whenever we needed his guidance and support, as he undoubtedly did for many others. He never considered helping others as a burden, but rather as a gift that he could gladly and freely offer.

Understanding who Lee was can help us comprehend how deep Carole Ann's loss was, and how dark her world became. For a very long time, she was unable to see joy or hope in her life. It was as if she had fallen into a deep chasm, where no light existed. Slowly, however, through the love of her family and friends, and through her faith, her life began to turn around.

As she looked back over her journey, Carole Ann saw that she had learned and adopted coping mechanisms and a deep understanding of the grief process: She had gone through the shock of diagnosis, the hope of a miracle, the acceptance of loss, and the loneliness and despair that came from losing such a special person.

Carole Ann also discovered that she was not alone in such grief, and it is with that realization that she threw herself into the writing of this book. Within its pages, she shares her fears and anxiety, her loss and her pain, and charts a path that she hopes will help others who are going through a similar loss. Her book is an honest portrayal of the processing of all the emotions, strategies, and strengths that any one of us must find to overcome such an assault on our soul. It is her hope that her insights may help others also find their way back, as she has. Carole Ann is again finding love and joy in her life. She has not finished the journey, but she has come a long way. Acceptance of such a profound loss does not mean that the pain is gone. The pain will always be there, but with time one is able to mitigate the pain and, again, find joy and happiness in family, friends, and the day-to-day events that shape our lives.

I will close by saying that my dear friend, Lee, whom I loved with all of my heart, would not want Carole Ann, or his family, to endlessly suffer the pain of his passing. His soul is a light that will always illuminate their path forward.

Mark Nitzberg, PhD, MD

ACKNOWLEDGMENTS

"What they never tell you about grief is that missing someone is the simple part."

—Gail Caldwell

In life, we weave a story of our journey here on this earth through various threads. These threads can be moments, people or experiences. They are the threads that tie together who we are and what our foundation looks like. Sometimes these threads are tattered and other times these threads are woven with strength. But no matter, they weave a history of the story of our lives.

I have written and re-written these acknowledgments several times. I felt there were so many people that I wanted to show my gratitude to, and with each acknowledgment that I would write, I would yet find the need to add another person whom I just had to recognize in this way. And so, the edits continued.

I have finally decided to write one collective and most heartfelt "thank you" to the absolute most wonderful people who helped me through my sorrow. People who truly held my children and I up as we were broken in our grief. These people collectively walked us through the darkness and guided us into the light, especially when we could not see the path ahead nor hear the sounds of the promises of life.

I look back at this time, and remember most gratefully the network of family and friends who truly carried us through this very emotional and difficult experience. Some brought meals, others brought flowers and so many just came to be with us in our grief, whether it was to sit by the side of my husband, or to just be with my family as best they could. I remember gifts, like garden memorial ornaments and a memorial quilt made out of my husband's work shirts. I remember a friend who bought us an air conditioner (because ours was not working properly) and then set it up in the room where my husband lay. I remember friends who helped to plan and orchestrate the funeral for Lee, gathering photos and putting together a beautiful program to hand out at the service, and I remember those who even participated in the actual service. I remember people of faith; a rabbi, a priest, a minister, a bishop and an Indian spiritual leader who all took the time over the course of Lee's illness to come to our house and pray with us and offer words of comfort and hope.

All of these people and specific acts of kindnesses and concerns represent the threads that held us together. There simply could never be enough words to show our sincere appreciation and humility for their tender mercies to my children, Lee and I. They have become a part of the story of my family's sorrowful encounter with cancer. As we look back on the years that we were struggling with so much sadness, there will always be the people, moments and experiences that will forever tie us together in this grief.

I also specifically want to acknowledge those who inspired me to write this memoir in the first place.

To my wonderful brother-in-law Bill Manning. While he succumbed to cancer only 3 years after Lee died, I want to say how much I love and respect him still. He stood by my side always and encouraged me to make good decisions and gave me the comfort of knowing that he was always there for me. I was like a bird with a broken wing, and he tenderly held me in his hands and tried every way he could to keep me from falling.

To my little angels, my grandchildren Willow Rose and Bodie Lee Baer, and to all the other little ones that will follow. They are the reason I put my thoughts and experiences into this book. They were not given the precious blessing of being able to grow up in the presence of their grandfather. I know they would have loved him and he would have loved them deeply and tenderly. I write this book for Lee's posterity, so that when they are older, they will understand a little more about who their Grandpa Lee was. Now they can only imagine him in Heaven, but I want them to know the incredible man that he was, not only professionally, but as a wise man of the greatest strength, kindness, humility and integrity.

To my dearest and most beloved children, David and Emily. My heart still aches for the pain that they have had to endure after losing their father. There was so much left in life for us to share together. So many more things we wanted to do. That was taken from us, but what remains in our hearts is immeasurable. They both carry their dad in them with such grace and dignity. And while he did not get to see our children as the adults they are today, he would be so incredibly proud of the world that they are making for themselves and their families. I can still see his shy smile as he beamed with joy when he talked about them, they were truly everything to him. We will continue on dedicating our lives in their dad's honor. We will find more ways to savor life, with more joys to follow. And our times in Bar Harbor will have even more profound meaning, for in some ways, he is still there, not just because this became his final resting place, but because in Bar Harbor, we have all experienced something magical. We hold dear in our hearts the sacred treasure that Bar Harbor is to our family. We all understand this on a very personal level.

I would also like to thank Barbie Wolfden and Virginia Teague for their initial editing of this book, and their encouragement that I could do this.

And finally, to the professionals at Archway Publishing for their dedicated guidance on this project.

OBITUARY

Lee Baer was born on August 24, 1955 in Brooklyn, New York. Upon graduating from the Brooklyn College of the City University of New York in 1977, he went on to pursue graduate study at Nova Southeastern University and obtained his Ph.D. in clinical psychology in 1980. He completed his predoctoral internship in psychology at the West Haven VA in Connecticut, and in 1981, he joined the Massachusetts General Hospital (MGH) as a Clinical Fellow in the Department of Psychiatry.

Throughout his tenure at the MGH, Lee served in various research, clinical, and teaching roles within the entire Harvard system. He worked on behalf of psychologists in a multitude of ways, from serving for 6 years as Director of Biostatistics in the MGH Psychiatry Department, to working as a psychologist and clinical consultant for the MGH out-patient and inpatient services and consultant to various pharmaceutical companies, and teaching as a Lecturer in the Harvard Psychology Department. Lee was promoted to Assistant Professor in 1986 within 5 years of joining the MGH, and became intimately involved in both the Psychology Training and Steering Committees. He played an integral role in the development of the core curriculum of the Cognitive Behavioral Scientist Track of the MGH internship in clinical psychology. He is known to dozens of cohorts of psychology interns as the leader of the Dissertation Seminar, which was a formal course designed to apply behavioral change principles to help interns complete their dissertations during internship year.

He co-founded the Obsessive Compulsive Disorder (OCD) treatment and research programs at both the MGH and McLean. His groundbreaking research on OCD symptom subtypes and his extensive empirical findings advanced behavioral and pharmacological treatments of OCD. Lee was a prolific writer, and published over 200 original peer-reviewed articles in the highest impact Psychiatry and Psychology outlets, including American Journal of Psychiatry, JAMA Psychiatry, and Biological Psychiatry. He is an internationally recognized leader in advancing the understanding and treatment of OCD. His work has been featured in major news outlets, and he has been honored for his research on OCD with a Lifetime Achievement Award from the International OCD Foundation.

A deeply caring clinician, Lee was universally liked and respected by his patients. His self-help book "Getting Control" was the first to describe a powerful behavioral treatment for OCD and his book "The Imp of the Mind" shed new light on the understanding and treatment of repugnant obsessions. His books have helped OCD patients and guided clinicians around the world for more than 20 years. His patients have gone out of their way to express the impact of his books by using words like "life changing," "saved my mind from torment", "gave me hope," and "powerful." Lee's patients have described him as "kind," "humble," "brilliant," and "playing a pivotal role in my recovery."

Driven by a personal mission to expand the reach of research on OCD and its treatment, in February 2010, Lee created a Twitter account and a website called "ocdandfamilies.org". His express purpose was to provide hope and help for patients suffering from OCD as well as their families. In particular, he was interested in disseminating information regarding taboo obsessions in OCD, which were lesser known to the general community. This platform enabled him to connect sufferers both locally and globally. He invited OCD sufferers, as well as psychology interns and fellows, to write guest blog posts on the website to normalize the experience of living with OCD and correct public misconceptions. In a related effort, Lee was the driving force in developing a website from which religiously scrupulous patients from the Jewish, Catholic, and Protestant traditions could seek information and help with their disorder. Together, these contributions highlighted his commitment to community outreach and education about OCD.

Beyond being an exceptional researcher and clinician, Lee will be remembered for having tirelessly supported and encouraged interns, postdoctoral fellows, and junior faculty. Lee's mentees have been very successful with publishing their papers, and presenting their research at professional meetings. They have also been thriving with respect to obtaining their own research funding and have been promoted to leadership positions within and outside the Harvard system. As a clinical supervisor, Lee conducted supervision with a cognitive behavioral style, asking Socratic questions and leading meetings with an agenda. He had been known to sit in on therapy sessions with his supervisees, and to downplay his clinical acumen by attributing his skills to years of experience. Lee was also an expert statistician and helped numerous trainees and faculty members with complex methodological questions.

Lee was dearly loved and admired by his colleagues at MGH. They have described him as kind, loving, forgiving, compassionate, generous of his time and talent, intellectually curious, and with the highest integrity and ethics. Given his talent and fame, he never lost that rare virtue, humility. As a clinician, there was no one more compassionate, empathetic, and respectful of his patients. No matter how difficult the patient or how complex the diagnosis, he never complained or gave up on a patient. He was a visionary and innovator, always in search of more effective treatments for his patients, especially the treatment resistant. Lee had a razor sharp mind but also a warm, humble, and caring style.

On July 27, 2017, Lee died at age 62 following a long battle with cancer. He is survived by his wife Carole Ann, his son David, and his daughter Emily.

Respectfully submitted,
Sabine Wilhelm, PhD, Professor of Psychology, Harvard Medical School, William E. Minichiello, EdD, Associate Professor of Psychology, Harvard Medical School, Angela Fang, PhD, Associate Professor, University of Washington

For last year's words belong to last year's language
And next year's words await another voice. …

And to make an end is to make a beginning.
T. S. Eliot, "Little Gidding"

PART ONE

1

THE DIAGNOSIS

But there was no need to be ashamed of tears, for tears bore witness that a man had the greatest of courage, the courage to suffer.

VIKTOR E. FRANKL, *MAN'S SEARCH FOR MEANING*

"You have cancer."

I remember the day we got the diagnosis. It was a typical day in our household. I was getting ready to head to Brandeis University where I taught evening dance classes, and my husband, Lee, was just returning from work at Mass General Hospital. He mentioned in passing that his back still hurt. He had had pain in his back for well over a month, but for some reason he hadn't made the appointment with his PCP to check out the source of the pain, even though he worked in a hospital. In my frustration, I decided to call out of work, telling him that I'd drive him to the ER. I wasn't nice about it either—I was that frustrated. We made the short drive to Newton-Wellesley Hospital, parked, and went into the emergency room. The ER was quite crowded—patients coming and going, some more emergent than others, children crying, nurses rushing about, doctors doing their thing—we waited a long time to be seen.

When Lee was finally seen, the doctor concluded that the source of his pain was a muscle he had pulled in his back, but just to cover all bases, he decided to do a few extra tests. A urine analysis showed that Lee had a small amount of blood in his urine. The young ER doctor told us that it seemed miniscule, but again "just to be sure," he would get an ultrasound as well.

After the ultrasound, we were asked to wait in the hallway on a gurney so that they could use the room for more urgent patients. I was bored, hungry, still frustrated, and eager to get home. We waited for an hour or so, watching patients come and go and witnessing the normal hustle and bustle of any ER. Then I saw our doctor coming towards us as he walked down the hallway. I could see that the look on his face was grim. I got a chill.

Please let him walk by us, I thought. I knew that look from having worked in an ER myself. *Let this guy be bringing the news he is carrying to someone else.*

He stopped at our gurney. He was pale and rather nervous. He told us that he saw a very large mass on my husband's kidney and had already spoken to Lee's primary care physician. Appointments had been made for us to see the PCP and an oncologist the following day. "This is urgent," he said.

While this was a shocking and unexpected piece of news, I wasn't too worried at this point. They called it an "incidental finding." Lucky that we caught it. I figured if it was kidney cancer, they would take out a kidney, my husband would have chemo and a bit of an interruption in his life, and then we would move on. One more cancer survivor.

The following day we met with Lee's PCP, who also happened to be my PCP, at Mass General Hospital. Dr. Weiss was a good man and had an amazing rapport with my husband—they were always joking together and had a real professional camaraderie. But this day, he wasn't joking. He was quite serious. My husband was light-hearted, and did not seem too worried, but then things got real when we were told, with all seriousness and sternness, that not only was the tumor in a kidney, but an even larger mass was in Lee's liver. As if the air had been sucked out of the room, I heard what was said but at that point I couldn't feel anything.

We then were sent to the next appointment with the renal oncologist, now both of us were in a dazed state of mind. The oncologist entered the room and introduced himself, and after reading Lee's chart, the first thing he asked us was "How old are your kids?" I thought, *He's asking the age of our kids so he can guide us how to appropriately tell them that their father is going to die.* Suddenly things were getting too much to bear, and then the bomb. "You have terminal cancer." The oncologist went on to say that Lee had about three to five months to live. He told us to cancel our upcoming family vacation to Florida because treatment needed to begin immediately. More air was sucked out of the room. We had no words. We just listened, unable to absorb what was said after that in any meaningful way. Neither Lee nor I could react. We were just breathing. Emotions gone. The ability to process anything, gone. Just one hour ago, our life was fine. Now this? I wanted to leave that cancer floor. I wanted to go home. Please just let me go home.

Our ride home was quiet. I held my husband's hand as he drove, but we didn't speak. We didn't cry, we didn't dare think. We just went home. All the while my sister had been texting me, trying to stay in the loop of what was going on. Through my texts to her, I could cry. I could scream. But I didn't react in front of Lee, not until I walked in the door of our house and found my sister, Susan, and my brother-in-law, Bill, waiting for us there. I fell to the floor, crying and sobbing. I couldn't stand. My body had no strength to bear the weight of this news. My sister got me up from the dining room floor and onto a chair, comforting me. Lee went to the couch in our family room, and my brother-in-law followed him. Neither said a word at first, and then I heard them talk about taking a ride together to pick up a prescription—Ativan. And the two of them left the house in total silence to head to the local CVS. I was glad that Lee had someone to go with him, for my body was not connected to my mind, and I had no ability to move. The strength to stand, to walk, even to move was gone.

I started to fall to pieces. How could life go from normal to this? How could our happy, predictable world suddenly be changing most horribly? How would I tell our kids? My son was in Barcelona on a study abroad, and my daughter was just a junior in high school. How could we do this to them? How could this be? We didn't invite cancer in, and now we had this permanent intruder. The thoughts flooded my mind, a whirlpool of fear, sorrow, disbelief and confusion. What was to become of us?

This is the story that answers that question, the story of my family's journey through an illness that swallowed up our lives and took away a beloved father, husband, son, brother, colleague and friend. It is a story of emotional chaos and shattered dreams, the story of being broken, being changed, but somehow finding how to live with the most devastating sorrow imaginable. It is a story about pain, loss, and profound grief, yet somewhere embedded in all of these things, it is a story about hope. For without hope, you have nothing.

2

THE DESPAIR

In times of grief and sorrow I will hold you and rock you and take your grief and make it my own. When you cry, I cry and when you hurt, I hurt. And together we will try to hold back the floods to tears and despair and make it through the potholed streets of life.

NICHOLAS SPARKS, *THE NOTEBOOK*

There is nothing in the world more tragic than despair. For despair offers no hope. Despair takes you in and shuts the light out, it deafens you, it blinds you, and it takes away your very breath. Despair promises only sorrow and devastation. Despair is the antithesis of hope. Yet, what despair takes away, hope gives back. And in this world, with all the difficulties that we may face, we must hold on to hope and let that light back in.

I learned very quickly what despair can do to you both physically and emotionally. In many ways, I was withering away along with my husband. I had to shut down emotionally and find the things that kept me going—friends, family, gardening, music—the things that often gave me hope and even a glimmer of sunshine. When my thoughts turned to the reality of our situation, as they often did, despair would get a hold of me, and I would feel myself crumbling. It was as if I was clinging on to the edge of a cliff with both hands tightly—the storm was in the distance, and the clouds were looming. And for a moment, I would want to let go—just let go and let it be. Fall apart. Fall down into the emotional abyss of despair. And then suddenly a tiny ray of light would permeate the darkness. Perhaps a friend sent us flowers, or maybe someone dropped off some comfort food or a sweet note. Oftentimes it would be my sister, Susan, bringing some homemade, healthy soup over, and then sitting with Lee while I went out on an errand. Maybe I'd see something as simple as a beautiful bird at my bird feeder, and the scene would bring a certain calm. That tiny ray of light would always break through, and somehow, I would find hope again.

In Victor Frankl's profound book *Man's Search for Meaning*, he asks the question, 'What happens when a man is stripped away of everything, what then remains?' His answer is that "what remains is the only true freedom we have as humans—the ability to choose our attitude given our current set of circumstances. The ability to choose one's own way." I found this so inspiring. I knew of course that I was not the only person in this world or universe to ever suffer a tragedy. I was among the thousands and even millions who have suffered immensely, were still suffering, or would suffer eventually. So who was I to feel "special" in my grief?

I watched as my husband tried and most days succeeded in making each day matter. His work became a valued source of comfort to him. The time he spent with our family became even more sacred. And what he wanted most, was normalcy, for the devastating disruption that a terminal cancer diagnosis brings upon one's life, most definitely takes away the gift of normalcy. I watched him take his pain and put it away on a shelf. It was still there, but he found ways not to let it dominate his precious living moments. While he could not escape the reality of his life, he chose his own way to push through each day. He chose to have an attitude of positivity and gratitude. And with each day little tidbits of happiness came through, moments of respite from the impending sorrow. I remember one Christmas when Lee, my sister-in-law, Andrea and I were standing there in the kitchen, and he very shyly said to us, "I have a Christmas present for you. The tumors shrunk." I remember his shy smile and tender, gentle voice. His tumors had shrunk. And so that day, that Christmas, we found some extra unexpected happiness. We took every morsel of happiness that we could get, and in that moment, it tasted of hope.

But the energy it takes to be positive and to have a good attitude, is still exhausting. It is not easy to be "okay" when your life is anything but okay. But as Lee always said, "What choice do we have?" He didn't want to see me cry, and he didn't want to waste time on the cancer that eventually would take his life. He wanted to focus on the Red Sox, the Celtics, and the Patriots. He wanted to enjoy barbecues and family gatherings. He wanted to choose his attitude and, as he said, "not let cancer define me." I can say I learned from the best. My husband, my partner, my mentor, and my companion was the best example of strength and endurance I could have asked for. Viktor Frankl would have been pleased.

I was learning to see life as it was in real time. Not perfect, not as I had hoped it would be, but still with moments of hope. Glimmering rays of sunshine—and when the sun did find its way to us, we basked in the warmth of that glow. Gratitude became an everyday word. Understanding the power of cherishing the very moment that we found ourselves in was also our daily task. Just live for now. Just breathe for today. Just be happy for this moment. Do not let the despair overshadow the day before us.

There were still many things to be grateful for, even though the despair was always there alongside the gratitude. And at that time, while we had no idea how long he would live, it turned out that Lee lived well over four years after the initial diagnosis. Even though we had first been told that he only had three to five months left to live. For while his initial cancer diagnosis was thought to be kidney cancer, it took three times for the professionals to get the diagnosis right: finally concluding that Lee had stage 4 neuro-endocrine cancer. The three to five months we were told he had to live turned out to be four plus precious years. Still as I look back over those years, I remember how challenging each day could have been if we let it. For each day brought the unknown, for we never knew if this was going to be the day when Lee's body started shutting down. So, when the feared final sorrow and despair did find its way in, when the cancer finally took my husband, it was in truth overbearing, even though we got more time than expected. There is never enough preparation for death. Letting someone go will never be easy, even with all the faith in the world. I truly do not think one can ever be fully prepared for the emptiness of losing a loved one. After my husband's passing, I remember crying so much that my eyes became infected. When I asked for an ointment to soothe the swelling, my dermatologist said that I simply needed to stop crying. Stop crying? Impossible. That would never happen.

The stretching and shaping of sorrow can take such an emotional toll on the body. But whilst we are in the midst of it all, we are growing. We are being changed, certainly against our will. Like a salmon swimming upstream against the current, we are forcing ourselves to succumb to nature and the natural course of things. Death is one of those things. And the strength that it takes to allow sorrow in is also profoundly powerful. Most importantly, it's okay to cry. It's okay to break. It's okay to hurt and see only darkness. But what is not okay is not to move through such pain. That is the task of grief, to allow it to come in and sit in your heart, feel it in every fiber of your being, and then find a way to let go of the despair, even if it takes years and years. Tenderly let that sorrow find an outlet, but do not let it capture your heart forever. Own your sorrow, own your pain, for it comes from a place of immense love and shared joys. As Kahlil Gibran has written, "When you are sorrowful look again in your heart, and you shall see that in truth you are weeping for that which has been your delight."

My husband was my delight. He was my source of comfort and calm. He always knew the answers to my questions, he was the voice of reason, and he was the wisest man I have ever known. His love for our family was profoundly deep and completely encompassing. We had a foundation and a bond that was truly powerful. Unfortunately, however, I did not know how lucky I was, often I criticized or complained about various things in our lives and our relationship, but I always knew he was a man of the utmost integrity; none could surpass him in that regard.

The despair and the sorrow and the pain were only because I had known the hope and the joy and the happiness that he afforded our family. Cancer took him away, yes; in that way it won, but it did not take away what was our delight. It could not take away our memories, our attitude, and especially our ability to endure through the most grievous time of our lives.

3

THE ENDURANCE

It had whispered to her, "Courage, dear heart."

C. S. Lewis, *The Voyage of the Dawn Treader*

In the aftermath of a devastating moment, a moment that suddenly re-defines the life we know, we are called to look deep inside ourselves and see exactly what makes us who we are. These are not moments that we want to stand against, but when faced with such adversity and sorrow, what else can we do? Perhaps it is not in the fullness of life, when we are smoothly moving along, that we need to completely understand the path we are on, but rather in those fragile, vulnerable moments when we know there is nothing else to lose. Growth, after all, usually comes when we are torn and twisted and stretched to our capacity, not when we are quietly and comfortably moving along. Growth takes pain and change and sometimes even immense sorrow.

The growth that I underwent changed me forever. I embarked on a journey of sorrow, but a journey that brought me to a greater under-standing of the necessity of enduring. This necessary endurance was my goal each day, it was the very reason I was able to face the tragedy upon us. What I would come to understand in the following years was that endurance was not a singular experience. It was not as if in one moment in time, the lesson on endurance and the ability to endure could be easily accomplished. I would come to understand that endurance was only possible through a myriad of experiences and commitments to endure, as well as with the collective people around me helping me to reach that hope. My ability to endure came from my faith, my family, and my friends, who held tight to my hand through this whole experience. This trial of cancer became the most significant learning experience in my life—but oh, my goodness, what a sorrowful lesson to endure. It forced me to face my beliefs, to dig deep down into my soul and to try to understand the universe that I found myself in.

Think for a moment about who you are, who you really are, and what you stand for. What makes you *you*? For me, I need to see the minuscule explanations, the lessons, the reasons to keep going. The journey I was about to take, this journey of terminal cancer, would afford me many experiences that forced me to take those deeper looks.

When I would ask my husband how he could endure the knowledge that he was going to die, he always replied, "What else can I do?" Then he would follow with, "It's not a problem until it's a problem." I had to digest those words over and over. Whether by our own accord or by a random act, we are always going to be stumbling upon problems in life. While some problems are far more serious and devastating than others, a problem, a moment of sorrow or fear or worry, is still a problem that we must face. It is not *if* we will get hit by something that hurts or tries to destroy us, but *when*. So endurance is something that we should understand, and by understanding endurance, we can stabilize our sorrows.

In his humble resolution to death, Lee taught me to endure. These were simple times for us. I learned to look at each day as another opportunity to be grateful. I learned that despite the terminal cancer that had so horribly intruded into our lives, the sun did not stop shining. The flowers still bloomed, the sky was blue, and there was beauty everywhere. Each moment was a treasure, despite this terminal diagnosis. I also appreciated the small things, like the tender act of holding my husband's hand while we perused the aisles of Home Depot. And I learned that we had two choices. One was to fall apart, which I was most inclined to do, and to sob and cry and scream to the world "Why us?" The other, which we as a family finally understood as the road we would take, was to endure this sadness. To stand together and take in the tender mercies that we had left. My husband always said never to ask "Why me?" Instead, he would gently say, "Why not me?" And so cancer was us. We had become a statistic, a page in the medical journals. But we were not going to let cancer define us, or not, as he said, until it was a problem.

Picture a willow in the field. It stands prettily amongst the wild gardens, offering a place for the bluebirds to perch. Quietly it reaches toward the sun in its efforts to grow. The rains bring it nourishment, the seasons strengthen its roots, and the winds test its spirit. As long as that willow can bend and sway as the mighty winds blow, it will endure. The insight I gained is that we too must bend and sway with life. So I would ask that you first find your roots, then find your sustenance—there you will find the ability to endure.

If our roots are firmly planted, then we can stand tall like the willow. What roots us? What gives us the ability to know who we are and where we are going? Perhaps we have been given religious or spiritual direction. Those who place their faith in God or a Higher Power may find that this faith allows their roots to grow steadfast. They understand their purpose on this earth, and they understand the concept of suffering. Others may plant their roots in a more scientifically substantiated notion and find that science gives meaning to their existence. Some balance the two, but both give us roots. In a moment of devastation—whether it be a cancer diagnosis, an unexpected disaster, or even a personal or emotional interference in our happy lives—our roots hold us steady. They link us to the earth and validate that we are a part of something bigger than ourselves.

My root system came from three things: my religious beliefs, my family, and my friends. All of these offered me a reason to endure. Oftentimes, when I found myself sobbing uncontrollably, my friends would tell me to lean on them if I could not bear the pain, to let them carry me through. And I did this very thing over and over. Their ability to hold me up helped me to hold my husband up. My dear friend Debby Wolfe would call me every morning just to check in. I would sob and sob, and she would listen and offer her kindness and love to me. That daily morning call became so important to me, more important than my friend may ever know.

It is also important in troubled times to understand that endurance does not mean unassailable strength. As the willow bends and sways in the harsh winds, so must we, but even willows can break. Bending and swaying for us might be having those moments when we allow ourselves to fall apart. And that is okay. Endurance, after all, is a journey, not a moment in time. Endurance is defined by everything associated with being strong—including falling down or falling apart. Endurance is getting back up and pushing forward. There is no limit on how many times we fall, but the important thing is to get up again. One reality is that once we are up, we may be broken and bruised, but this is not failure—it is strength. It is growth. We are still reaching for the sun to make us taller, even in our pain. Yet for some, getting up again may feel almost impossible. And while the desire to endure might be present, the ability to do so may be unattainable, no matter how hard we try. For those of you who feel this way, I would suggest, as I did myself, to seek professional support. A professional can help you find a way to move forward on your own terms. This too, is indeed a path of endurance.

Throughout this time that turned into four years of added life, we still had laughter, we still had hopes and dreams, and we still experienced growth. The sad reality was that this cancer would take my husband's life at some point, but did this knowledge help us cherish each day more? Yes, it most certainly did. We did not have the gift of time, nor did we pretend that there would be some miraculous cure—although, of course, that was always somewhere in our minds. Often, I would feel that we walked around with a horrible neon sign over our heads: HE HAS TERMINAL CANCER. Still, simple things like trips to the grocery store seemed more enjoyable, doing laundry and seeing my husband's clothes still there in the washing machine was comforting and the TV shows we watched were funnier, sadder, or more interesting. My husband's presence was a continued gift in our home. His footsteps were sweet music, and hearing him click away on his computer reassured me that he was still here, living amongst us. And we tried, oh how we tried, to just be normal again. The "new normal" as we called it, was always accompanied by sorrow. Cancer and sorrow were our constant companions. But we endured even to the end. Honestly, what else can you do when there is no other way?

The sustenance it takes to endure life's sorrows is like the very marrow in our bones. It is in a way our life source. The food that keeps us going. What are we made of? What gives us the strength to endure? When we are asked to find inspiration to live despite the hardships we face, profound and personal values take on new meaning and power. Where does enrichment come from? What do you feed your soul from? This sustenance is like the air we breathe—we cannot really see it, but it is there, and without it we would wither away.

In our weakest moments, when we cannot stand, when we feel the winds will break us permanently, we must dig deep. What holds us together emotionally? What are our convictions? What brings us peace in this world? That is what we must seek. For there will be times when the wind is at a hurricane force, when all that surrounds us and all that matters to us is blown and tossed to a fate that is not in our control. How do we endure and sustain the sorrow, the fear, and the absolute soul-wrenching reality of death? I asked myself this a million times. I often thought that I would lose the battle and that I myself would be destroyed. If I had let myself slip into the depths of doubt and fear, I might never come back. I *had* to endure. For my children. For myself. And for my husband, who needed to see that we would be okay even when he was no longer here.

As I reflect back on this time of sorrow, I see that our family was held together by the sustenance we had in our lives at this time—a time of the most unbearable vulnerability. When someone offered to hold me up, despite my independent nature, I allowed myself to accept that help. My children, too, were lucky: their lives were very busy, and their father and I wanted this normalcy for them, for their lives to be stable, and so they found ways to endure and sustain their emotional strength. I cannot emphasize enough the immense gratitude we all had for people who walked us through such a dark tunnel, where oftentimes we could not see that light would ever find its way in to our lives again. Yet we are all made of something that perhaps we do not even know is there. I call it a life force—that amazing human quality that seeks survival even in the darkest times. This life force lies within each of us. This life force is sacred. It is the blood that flows through our veins, and that very life force is what keeps us going.

During the years that my family lived and breathed cancer, we learned about what our life force was. And while this may all sound very simple, it was far from simple. It was beyond difficult. Our energy was always at risk of being sucked into this vacuum of cancer. Yet there was no other way for us. We wanted to endure. We wanted to have hope. We wanted to push through and be normal again, or at least feel normal, even if that meant significant denial. Cancer was always "the thing" that lingered about in our hearts and minds, but we didn't want to think about it too much, because if we didn't invite it in, maybe it would stay away. But it never left us. Our hearts were always heavy, our eyes told a story of pain, and our family just had to hold strong. We chose to endure the best we could.

The life force we held on to was our family bond. At the end of the day, it was for us the love we had for one another. Love goes a long way. Love strengthens. Love endures. And for us it was, is, and always will be what holds us together. Even now, seven years since my husband left us, we still feel that love. While cancer took away my husband, Lee still remains in our hearts. Love is eternal, and love will help us continue to endure eternally.

4

THE JOY

I don't think of all the misery, but of the beauty that still remains.

ANNE FRANK, *THE DIARY OF A YOUNG GIRL*

If you believe that life has a purpose, then how do you find that purpose? Perhaps it is to learn, to be kind, to do good—and then hopefully to find joy. But finding joy through pain is quite difficult. However, as with anything lost, while you may not find or see it, doesn't mean that it isn't there. I knew innately that somewhere life still held happiness, there was still goodness, and somewhere someone was still laughing and smiling, even if it wasn't me at the time. I knew that if indeed there was a God, He would want us to be happy, to know joy no matter what. Goodness knows that was what I had been taught, but maneuvering this idea around in my mind, when all I could eat and drink was sorrow, was almost an impossible notion. Joy. Would I ever know joy again? Would my beloved husband ever know joy again somewhere in the heavens? Would my children ever know joy again? I simply didn't know.

What is joy, after all? It is, I think, an intangible emotion deep in one's soul. I don't know if you can wake up and say, *Today I will be joyful.* I'm not sure you can convince your body and intellect as well as your heart to just decide to be joyful. But I do think, and this comes back to Viktor Frankl's notion that we can choose our attitude, that we can choose happiness, and in doing so, joy will come and softly, quietly, and without even disturbing the air we breathe, find us. And the immense depth of joy that we are capable of feeling will overcome us and give meaning to even the most tragic of circumstances. Joy, then, should also be our motivation while we are here on earth.

In the days, weeks, and months leading up to my husband's liver failure, I continued doing what I usually did. I still worked. I tried as best as possible to keep life normal for my family, as did my husband. He went to work and had outings with friends. We even traveled—we actually made that Florida vacation after all that we had planned before the diagnosis. We knew that Lee's cancer was slowly overtaking his organs and that one day he would start to go into failure, but we tried to go on as normally as possible. Cancer was not a frequented subject in our house, even though it was ever-present, hovering over us like a vulture about to pounce. What I tried to focus on then was my spirituality. I wasn't mad at God—I fully understood and accepted the nature of things—but what I needed was the assurance that He was there somehow in our midst. I focused more closely on the principles of many of the great philosopher's and prophet's teachings and on the importance of bringing those principles into my life.

I knew also that my children were watching me in this time of my life. They were watching me as I tried my best to be strong for my family. A very dear friend, David Harding who himself had lost his wife at a young age, said to me that with grief there was no way around it. You just had to move through it. The thought was almost impossible. I didn't want to move through grief. I wanted to wake up and see that this was all a dream. But his words stuck with me. I understood that even though there would be a painful ending, a moment when my family would be devastated, the best way to move through this cancer was to find whatever joy still remained out there. I also knew in my heart that it was a promise from God. He wants us to have joy everlasting. My sorrow was perhaps a part of this existence, and while I cried daily, I did my best to find the joy.

What brought us joy were things like cuddling on the couch and watching a good TV show. Lee loved *The Big Bang Theory*, so we watched it often. He loved to barbecue, and so we enjoyed delicious family meals cooked on the barbecue. He loved his children passionately, so as we always had done, but even more intently, we cherished every moment with them and gloried in their lives and all the things they were doing. The things that were common in most lives became magnified in ours. These were simple times, but the joy was there.

If I were to speak to someone who is in pain or suffering for any reason at all, I would tell them to seek joy. Pleasure is momentary, but joy is eternal. Joy fills our veins with the peace and calm needed to right any ship. In my sorrow and pain, I also realized that even though our outcome was pretty much assured, there was still the possibility of joy. If joy is in your inner being, you can find refuge from the external failures of life. Joy is about a way of being, a way of promising your soul to learn to understand what matters. I wanted my family to live in joy, even though my husband was ill. I wanted us not to waste time on the things we couldn't change and just focus on the fact that we had another day. Lee wanted that too. And so in the craziest of ways, we had joy, because we still had each other.

Nothing ever came easy, though—joy takes commitment. It is a heavenly characteristic, a heavenly goal. I would often hear how trials and tribulations were part of understanding joy in its deepest meaning. Scriptures say to take your trials and tribulations and be patient and count the experience as joy. "Count it all joy"? "Be patient in tribulation"? This seemed preposterous. How could my family see the trial we were suffering, the trial that my poor husband was enduring, as joyful? Oh, my goodness. At first that thought annoyed me. Joyful in trials? Come on. I understood the thought of being patient in tribulation—I understood that when you can't change something for the better, like miraculously curing cancer, you find ways around it, and you must look for the good in things. But be joyful in your trials? Our hearts can only take so much.

But then I came to understand the very power of joy that one arrives at in an extreme emotional state. As with a positive attitude, your body responds to uplifting thoughts. Joy somehow blankets the sorrow; it covers the pain in a very subtle way. It cannot obliterate the sorrow or pain, but it can hold you like a mother comforting a child in her arms. Joy embraces you softly and tells you, "It's okay to cry, but I am here." Joy helped us to have hope that whatever life had to offer us, we still had experienced joy. And even when we would suffer the most devastating sorrow, joy's arms would still hold us and do her best to comfort us. I understood that joy would not abandon me, as long as I reached out for her.

What I chose to do, truly, was to make each day count. When the sun shone brightly, I basked in it. When it rained, I was grateful that it watered my flowers. I chose to look at the colors of life as majestically as the most exquisite tapestry. And while every day was still filled with moments of sorrow, I worked very hard to find the happy moments in it.

Then there was fear. My enemy was fear. When fear took over, it was a long climb back to my emotional safety zone. Joy did not recognize fear—but fear was also my constant companion, lingering by my side, waiting to invade my emotional space. I tried my best to keep fear at bay so that joy could thrive. It was as if I had a sacred garden in which I planted the seeds of hope and faith. Joy was the water and the nutrients that kept my garden growing strong. Fear was the darkness that did not let in the sunshine and was the great destroyer of all things. What joy is to survival, fear is to complete devastation.

5

THE FEAR

Scared is what you're feeling. Brave is what you're doing.

EMMA DONOGHUE, *ROOM*

I am afraid of the dark. I'm afraid of coyotes. I'm afraid of scary movies. So, I usually leave a night-light on, I'm careful where I walk my dogs and I don't watch scary movies. That sort of "fear" is in my control. If I'm afraid of something—if at all possible, I avoid it. But what happens when something you fear presents itself in a way that you can't avoid it? When the thing you fear isn't going to go away, what do you do? Cancer is that monster that hides in your closet, sneaks under your bed, and pops out of nowhere. I think we all fear cancer, or more specifically, we fear death. No one wants to die. We want to live. There is never enough time to be here on earth, even if there is a heaven. Earth is where we want to be.

While my husband did not want to talk about his cancer, I had to talk about it to anyone who would listen, especially my closest friends. My fears about what all of this would look like were unbearable—and if I was to hang on to any sort of positivity, I had to face this fear. Talking about it was a way to face it. I was grateful for the sympathetic listening ear of a dear friend. I hung on to the bits of wisdom and encouragement

I received. At this time, I couldn't stand fully on my own, so I leaned on those I trusted, and we faced this fear as a team.

Yet, as I look back, I realize that I did look at this cancer head on, even though I didn't know it. I faced it with every fiber of my being. Yes, I was terrified of it—I dreaded waking up because the whole horror show would start all over again—but I faced it. I have learned that there is no right or wrong way to do this. Our coping skills should develop naturally, as long as they are built upon a healthy foundation, and not be forced. How we manage this devastating pain falls heavily on our survival skills. In the midst of cancer or even some other devastation, we are weakened. Our spirits are fragile, and so how one copes is how one copes. No judgment and no apologies. For me, grief wasn't and isn't linear. At my absolute weakest moments, I still knew that I wanted to rise above the pain and sorrow. Fear was not going to lock me up and take me away to some distant emptiness. I had to look this straight in the eye, accept my pain, accept my sorrow, accept my fear, but not let it kill me too. There were going to be too many casualties in all of this anyway.

Being afraid, falling apart, and wanting to give up on life is not failure at such times. We are allowed to break, and everyone who knows me saw how my heart broke. What *is* failure is allowing fear and sorrow to overcome us and take away our ability to know that life is still worth living. We win when we fully understand that joy can prevail; it can win over fear. And most important, a broken heart or a shattered soul doesn't mean we are not "okay." They were a part of my journey of cancer. It's okay not to be okay—just keep remembering that.

There is a dubious challenge when we face death. There is nothing about it that is easy, even if one has a strong religious faith. I believe in God, and therefore I believe that we go on, that all that is promised of a beautiful existence in the afterlife can be. But even that belief was challenged. When fear took hold of me, I asked the wrong questions, and I let doubt dominate my thoughts. *We go on, right? Well, do we go on? There is an afterlife, right? Well, is there an afterlife, I mean really?* All these thoughts became scrambled in my head. What I believed or didn't believe didn't change anything. My beliefs were not going to change my husband's cancer, nor would it change the eternities, whether it is there or not. So I had to let go, breathe, and just let things be. The task of managing sorrow was enough—I couldn't solve the mysteries of the world. The Dalai Lama said it best: "If you have fear of some pain or suffering, you should examine whether there is anything you can do about it. If you can, there is no need to worry about it; if you cannot do anything, then there is also no need to worry." This was the lesson I was meant to learn in this moment of my life: how exactly not to worry. I was learning that if you cannot change something, don't fight it. I was a student, and my teacher was my husband; through his cancer, we had many lessons to learn. He understood when to worry and when not to worry, and although it didn't change his pain, he did not fear cancer. Lee would not let cancer define him, and so he did not let fear define him.

Yet the horrible nightmare did finally come. Late one evening, my son and daughter and I were there with him, just us. All our dear friends who had stopped by to visit during the day had gone, my daughter's three best friends Jamie, Leah, and Ava, whom he loved dearly had just left about an hour before things started to change. Lee started breathing in such a strange way that it scared me. I later learned it was called agonal breathing. I called the hospice center. The hospice worker said she couldn't come because her shift was about to end. I would have to wait until the next person started their shift. My mind went blank. I wanted to scream at her, "But he's dying! What do I do?" Instead, I called the ambulance, something that Lee had asked me not to do. But I was afraid. So afraid. My son texted my sister and nephew, though I did not know it at the time. My daughter was there somewhere in the room, but I saw only my husband.

The ride to Emerson hospital was something I have chosen to forget. What roads did we travel? Was there traffic? How were the ambulance people when they carried Lee out of his house for the last time? I was blank. My heart was beating, but it wanted to stop. I was sobbing inside, but I stayed stoic.

When we got to the hospital, as soon as I came out of the ambulance, I saw my sister and nephew. Their faces were pale. I was so glad they were there. My sister could be my voice, for at that point I had no words other than the thought *Just please don't let him die*. But I knew this was it. And it was. My precious, wonderful husband was leaving this earth, and all I could do was watch. We were brought very respectfully into a private room in the ER, where we all—my daughter, my sister, my mother, and I—gathered around Lee's gurney. My poor son could not bring himself to enter the room where my husband was lying—he was too traumatized and broken. But I remember David sitting there in the hallway on a chair just across from our room, with his face down, and my nephew, Ian, right beside him. This simply did not seem real. But this moment had come. Morphine was administered and I held Lee's hand until his last moment and soon felt his hold weaken.

Please, please, please wake me up from this nightmare. The emergency room was quiet that night. I remember the kindness of the nurses and doctor, who were respectfully silent as we buckled in sorrow when my husband took his last breath. One nurse told me she had never been so moved. The hospice people called the ER, and I heard my sister tell the doctor not to let them speak to me. She explained how they had responded when I called them, and the doctor was shocked. But all of that didn't matter now. I heard something about donating organs, but all of that sounded too much to bear. Yes, donate them, as was his wish. I wondered where would they take him. I just wanted to take him back home, alive and well. How could this be? Then we left, devastated to leave him there without us.

I simply could not believe this was happening, even though I had known for four years that one day it would. When we left the hospital that sorrowful night, it felt so cold and chilly, even though it was July. The drive home was impossible. I never felt so alone in all my life. Where did he go? Oh, my goodness, where did he go?

In the next few days, some of my dearest friends came to the house and helped put together the service, for I had no strength to do so. They gathered pictures and put together a program. I chose the music, had some of his closest friends help with the eulogy, and I myself prepared a few words. But still, I could not believe the emptiness.

The funeral was a sacred experience, for while our hearts were shattered, the words spoken in his honor were profound and full of love and respect. My dear friend Kevin Rollins conducted and my beloved friend Julie Marriott played the piano. Two women from my church sang the song "For Good" from the play Wicked. I still remember the words of those who spoke: my dear friend, David Harding who had lost his wife to cancer; two of Lee's very close friends, Mark Nitzberg whom he had gone to grad school with, and Bill Minichiello with whom he had worked at Mass General Hospital; my sister Susan; and my daughter Emily, who read a poem that left most of the chapel in tears. The poem was something about him being there when she took her first breath, and she being there when he took his last.

And so it was done. The journey of cancer came to an end. And though my husband's journey on this earth had ended, we had to continue. But I did not know how.

6

THE PAIN

Do not go gentle into that good night,
Old age should burn and rave at close of day;
Rage, rage against the dying of the light.

DYLAN THOMAS, "DO NOT GO GENTLE INTO THAT GOOD NIGHT"

No one, in my opinion, is ever really prepared for death. I could never have imagined the depth of the heartache of my husband's passing until after it happened, even though I had known that his death was imminent. There was very little left of me when Lee died. I was emotionally distraught and physically drained. My body and soul had been left depleted. My heart ached—I fully understood what "heartbroken" meant, because my heart felt as if it had been shattered into a million pieces. I could not see the way out of this pain. There was simply no medicine that could calm my sorrows or ease my tears. I was overwhelmed with grief. My body literally went into a type of shock, my blood labs went wild, and I developed an arrythmia, vertigo and tinnitus. I wanted to fade away. I just didn't want to hurt this much. It was too hard to live.

To Dylan Thomas's poignant exhortation to "rage, rage against the dying of the light," I can honestly say I tried. My family tried, and my friends tried. Even at the last minute we were offered a complimentary flight to the Mayo Clinic in Minnesota, where the doctors could perform a liver dialysis. I remember our son and daughter being so eager to have this morsel of hope, but alas, it was determined that Lee was too far into liver failure. At first my children refused to believe that the doctors said that he would not be a candidate after all. My heart broke even more to see their profound disappointment at knowing that this would have been our last chance, for we were running out of time. We did not want to give up until we had to, and that time came on July 27, 2017.

I had received countless books from my friends that offered profound insights into how to manage this time of my life. I read those books with voracity, trying to find the answer to my pain. There were so many incredible words of wisdom, but none that could stop my pain. I heard stories of others who lost their partners and maneuvered through their grief with such strength and faith, yet I couldn't find my strength, and my faith became weak. Not so much because I stopped believing in God, but because my pain just took over every aspect of my thinking. All I could do, quite literally, was to breathe sorrow. When I look back at the person I was then, I can still feel that sorrow in every pore of my body.

In some ways, the pain protected me from being angry. I was so engulfed by my sorrow that there was no room for anger. I understand that everyone experiences and emotes grief very differently, but in a way I am glad that anger did not accompany me in those moments. I would always remember my husband's words: if you can't change something, don't fight it. I wasn't fighting the world or fate because such a tragedy had fallen upon our family, I was simply sobbing for this tragedy that left its mark on our lives.

Cancer took my husband away. My life was empty. My world was shattered. My heart hurt with every beat it took. Pain became my constant companion. I learned that this vast hole in my life would change me forever. While I could not escape the darkness that chased out the light, I learned that I had something in me that kept me going. I had no choice if I still wanted to live here amongst this world. I came to understand that I would be in terrible pain all the time. I had to accept my own fate, accept my own pain, which had become my unwanted companion.

The acceptance did not come with ease, nor with composure, but with real tears and sorrow that I wore on my sleeve every day. It was just who I had become in this moment of grief. I could not avoid my sorrow; I could not pretend that I was okay. And honestly, I didn't want to pretend that I was okay, because I simply wasn't.

There were many moments where I was called upon to exhibit strength, and most times I was able to do so, but that wasn't always the case. I remember one Sunday morning, when I was asked to say an opening prayer in my church during our sacrament meeting, I politely asked if I could pass. But the person who had asked me said it was okay if I was sad—he wanted me to say the prayer anyway. I went to the pulpit, and I cried throughout the prayer, barely able to get the words out. I couldn't help it. I could barely speak the words asking God to bless us all that day, to guide and strengthen us, but I managed to get through despite my pain. I am sure God knew of my sorrow that morning, as I know He knows all of our sorrows. As James Jones wrote in *From Here to Eternity*, I knew pain! I knew how hard it was to face the day, and how precious the night was for me because it was then that I could fall asleep and forget the pain within me.

7

THE EMBRACE

What cannot be altered must be borne, not blamed.

Thomas Fuller

In the days, weeks, months, and years that followed, we of course had to accept this loss. Never has a day gone by when Lee is not on our minds, in our memories, or a part of how we make decisions as a family. I show my grandchildren pictures of Grandpa Lee, as my granddaughter calls him. She knows he is in heaven, but she is still not sure where that is. But we push on, for there is no other way through this sort of darkness.

For the last four years and five months of Lee's life, we had endured, hoped, and tried our best to get through a terrible time. We focused on life and tried our darndest to live each day to the fullest. I cannot emphasize enough, however, that while my message is endurance through strength and hope, through joy and positivity, embracing this fate was also accompanied by sorrow, despair, and fear. Being afraid did not mean that the day was not full of positivity. Feeling joy did not mean that we were not suffering in the depths of despair. And though we endured, our hearts were still full of sorrow. All these emotions came to exist somehow in harmony with one another. And this is how it was—a polarized array of emotions learning to live under one roof, in one human soul.

What nourished us and fed the things that strengthened us was our family and friends. That was paramount. But it was also our decision to stay focused on the day. All we could see was today. Looking back or looking forward had no benefit. The day at hand was all we had. It was as if we knew that today would be magical. And when I started with ruminations— "What if?" or "If only" and more often "Why us?"—I knew they needed to be quelled, like putting out a campfire. Those thoughts were dangerous to my emotional being. One negative thought could take hold of me and burn through my defenses in a way that could be devastating.

The act of enduring in the face of death is strenuous. The effort is emotionally exhausting. But as Lee always said, "What other choice do we have?" I listened to him and followed his cues. This was a horrible, horrible time in our lives, but despite it all, we had to endure.

The sorrows and disappointments in life will find us, absolutely and without doubt. So it is not that we won't have grief and difficulties; it is how we respond to these. We can be furious at fate, as I was; we can doubt our beliefs, as I did; and we can even start to resent fate—those moments are allowed when we are in pain. But then comes the final act of endurance, and that is our response to grief and sorrow. If I could give one gift of advice, a morsel of wisdom from someone who was so broken that I thought I'd never stand again; we must look trials and tribulations directly in the eye. Believe in that one bit of strength that you have. It is there, I promise you.

8

THE KINDNESS

To live is to suffer, to survive is to find some meaning in the suffering.

FRIEDRICH NIETZSCHE

As I look back, I remember the many times someone reached out to me through this devastation. I remember so desperately needing their support. I remember that my days were so clouded in tears, and my nights were so clouded in darkness, that oftentimes I could not appreciate the people who were there for me. I did not understand that the act of kindnesses that I experienced on a day-to-day basis was necessary to my healing. I also remember a moment when I said to a dear friend, "I can't do this." And she said so tenderly, "Then I will carry you through this until you can." And she did.

Grief pulls us inward. It puts us in a corner where we want to hide and shrivel up and fade away, because the pain and sorrow is simply too much for a soul to endure. Grief holds us down and holds us back from the world. And even though my crying and lamentations were certainly very public, my grief took me to a very dark place that was very lonely. I would look around and see my friends with their husbands, other children with their fathers, old couples with their partners, and I just didn't see where I fit in anymore. I was confused with my identity, or my place. I despised (and still do) the word "widow."

Yet even as grief was trying to pull me in deeper and deeper, I understood that life was important. I understood that my children still deserved to be happy in their endeavors and that I needed to breathe more steadily for them. In the appropriate time it took, I began to see that I wasn't the only one suffering in this world. There was suffering everywhere: wars, murders, illnesses, loneliness, hunger … people suffer all the time, unfortunately, and I was not unique. As I processed my sorrow, I realized that in the same way that a lifeline was extended to me by people's kindnesses, I needed to do the same. I started to get involved again in the philanthropic organizations I belonged to. My eyes slowly started to see the world around me again, and I realized I was still needed—and more important, being needed meant that I was still alive.

Just as grief had kept me hidden under a blanket of sorrow, service became the light that found its way back into my life. The small and large acts of kindnesses that brought me out of the devastating singularity I was feeling, helped me to see that I was becoming a part of humanity again. And seeing that I was not alone in my suffering made me feel I had a responsibility to pass on the experiences of my own suffering, in the hopes of helping someone else going through their own pain. By becoming aware that I might make a difference in someone else's life, I could give meaning to my suffering and a purpose to my pain. Suffering brings growth through enduring and moving through one's pain, and then it opens the valley of emotions and empathy so that there is profound meaning again in what we do.

Like those around me who helped pull me through the darkness by being priceless beams of light, I wanted to become a part of that light and in turn pull someone else through their darkness.

9

THE HEALING

Let there be spaces in your togetherness,
And let the winds of the heavens dance between you.
Love one another but make not a bond of love:
Let it rather be a moving sea between the shores of your souls.
Fill each other's cup but drink not from one cup.
Give one another of your bread but eat not from the same loaf.
Sing and dance together and be joyous, but let each one of you be alone,
Even as the strings of a lute are alone though they quiver with the same music.
Give your hearts, but not into each other's keeping.
For only the hand of Life can contain your hearts.
And stand together, yet not too near together:
For the pillars of the temple stand apart,
And the oak tree and the cypress grow not in each other's shadow.

KHALIL GIBRAN, *THE PROPHET*

My husband and I loved this quote from Khalil Gibran. We even had the last few sentences on our wedding invitation when we married in 1990. I think now that our togetherness almost always had those spaces—spaces that allowed for growth and individuality. At the same time, we were two pillars, as the quote says, holding up the temple—two souls on this earth, holding up our lives that we built together. Death, however, was the ultimate distance, the ultimate moving sea between our two souls. It is ironic to me that this quote has taken on such a meaning so different from what I felt when I first read it so many years ago. But isn't that how life is? We understand meaning in different ways at different times in our lives.

As I write, it has been almost seven years since the passing of my beloved husband. It has been a time of profound growth amidst profound pain—a time when I learned that I could either retreat from humanity or find a way again to exist with meaning. I found that the darkness cannot overtake us if we continually reach for the light. And I don't mean this in a frilly, shallow way—we *must* find that light, whatever it is, to overcome the darkness that engulfs us when we are in so much pain.

Then, as my family was finding our way again and trying our best to heal and find our footing, we suffered another unexpected devastation. While we were in the deepest throngs of sorrow, my wonderful and dear brother-in-law, Bill, also passed away from cancer, only fifty-three years old and just three years after my husband had passed away. My brother-in-law's death was a sorrow placed upon sorrow, of heartbreak compounded by heartbreak. My sister and I would look at each other in absolute stunned, incredulous pain, and say, "Really, God? Both of them?" To lose both of these precious fathers and husbands in just three short years was beyond belief. It was as if we could not run from sorrow. Unbeknownst to us, while my brother-in-law was promising my husband on his deathbed that he would care for my family and continue to guide us through our life and important decisions, he himself had terminal colon cancer. My husband had no idea that Bill was soon to follow the same path. And while I was being comforted by my sister, I had no idea that I would soon be comforting her in turn. Some things in life you just can't make up.

And so, through the terrible and unfortunate passing of two very dear loved ones, I have moved through various stages of grief, returned to various stages of sorrow, and ultimately found a place for this devastating pain. I have come to understand that one simply does not "heal"—at least I haven't in the usual definition of the word. By "healing," I do not mean that I have resolved the passing of my husband nor the subsequent passing of my brother-in-law in any way that will ever bring real closure. I think it is hard to have closure when someone dies; the hole in one's existence cannot be mended and that sorrow just becomes a new way to breathe. I breathe sorrow in some ways every day, but I am finding a way to live again and finding the joy that living can bring. What I mean by healing is an understanding that life matters, even though many times I felt it didn't. I came to understand that the very precious breath we have is a gift on all levels. And through our grief, we need to believe that the process, while it is different for all of us, strengthens us if we let it. Sorrow has no rules, and grief has no exact guidelines that we must follow. There are simply no right or wrong paths on the road to healing except to be guided by hope.

My suggestion in your journey to healing would be to find strength and inspiration in whatever means you can. Allow the tears to flow and your heart to break. Be kind and gentle with your pain, and be forgiving of others when they do not understand your pain. But never lose hope, and never doubt your ability to endure what seems insurmountable. The human soul is powerful. Find this power within you, even if it may take some time. Rumi, also known as Jalāl al-Dīn Muḥammad Rūmī, a Persian poet of the thirteenth century and Islamic scholar, said, "The wound is the place where the Light enters you." This very light will be your strength. The heavens do not want you to be broken. If your loved one were somehow there beside you, they would say, "Find your way. It will be okay." Finding one's way, in whatever grief you are suffering from, must be what you seek. While sorrow can break you, hope can lift you. While suffering can break you, endurance can lift you. And while despair can break you, love can lift you.

10

THE LIGHT AHEAD

No man ever steps in the same river twice, for it is not the same river and he's not the same man.

HERACLITUS

In life, what may seem like the end may not really be so. For only death is truly the end here on earth, and even that is considered a new beginning by many. I slowly came back to life, pulled by the lives of my children, my family, my friends, and my church. I continued to cry, even sob, everywhere I went. I cried at grocery stores. I cried at birthday parties. I cried at church. I even put cry emojis on any text I sent. I wasn't ready to stop crying. I cried all the time. But I wanted to heal. I wanted to find a way through the sorrow. I had no idea what that would be, or how I would do it. I just wanted to know what it felt like to be okay again—to feel normal, to enjoy life again.

Healing for me came in many ways. Time was the most profound journey through this sorrow, along with the ability to realize that life still offered happiness. The sorrow I felt had to walk hand in hand with the happiness I had hoped would return. I had to accept that in every part of my body, I would always feel some sort of sorrow, some sort of profound loss. I also had to accept, and most importantly *allow*, happiness to come into my life again. It was a new way of being. If the loss of my husband was like losing a limb, this new way of thinking was my prosthesis. I was basically learning to walk again.

Another very important experience I had on this path to healing was a grief group that I joined at Newton-Wellesley Hospital, led by Catherine. She was my lifesaver. She let me feel the pain as I needed to, and she understood the grief that all of us in that support group were trying to move through. To this day, I know God put her in my life. She was paramount in my healing. And she helped me to see that life could be okay again, even as I learned to walk without the limb that was my husband. This grief group was so therapeutic, and so touching, that I longed for it each week. It was strengthening to be in the presence of people who tragically were suffering as I was. We shared our grief and held on to one another emotionally as we moved through the sorrow. Week by week, bit by bit, we got stronger. That group offered hope when all we knew was despair, and that hope was priceless.

Amid my sorrows, one of the greatest gifts that the universe gave to me, just by chance, was finding a companion who also had his share of sorrow. I wasn't looking to meet anyone; as a matter of a fact, I still felt very married to my husband. But I was empty, and I was lonely. This person entered my life in the most unexpected way. He lived in Florida and was someone I knew when I was still in college and he was at Harvard Medical School. Roberto was someone I had not been in touch with in over four decades. By him living in Florida, and me living in Massachusetts, the connection felt safe. I knew there would be no pressure to "date" or meet for dinner, because the distance prevented that, and so it made our talks feel "safe." After a year of talking by phone and processing our individual grief, we found that we had unexpectedly and tenderly fallen in love. The depth of our respect for each other, as well as the ability to fulfill the hole in each other's hearts, was a tender mercy. It was as if the universe said, "Okay, you have suffered enough. Here is someone to help carry you through life." To this day I feel that his love actually brought me back to life, and with all the sorrow I carried, I suddenly had a place for happiness too. I felt some guilt in finding happiness again, but as my dear friend Debra Kaye said to me, "One light does not outshine the other." And so I have had the gift of these two beautiful lights who found their way into my life and became a significant and important part of my journey on this earth. I am in absolute awe and appreciation that both men graciously allowed me to be part of their journey too, and I am deeply humbled. They are equally gifted human beings, now sealed to me in my eternal perspective.

So new beginnings can be anything. Whatever they may be; a special person, a new job, a new perspective, or whatever it is that shows you another way to breathe again, showing you that what you thought was an ending can lead to another path. And while sorrow may never be far at hand, happiness and life is there, waiting for you to take hold of it. There can be a light ahead, even if you can't always see it. New beginnings can be anything that fills that emptiness, let these new beginnings breathe life into your heart, allowing the flow of light again.

I still breathe sorrow each day. I still find moments of pain and feel that I will break again. I have come to understand that this sorrow will never leave me; it is just there now, a part of who I have become. But I also live in a world where I understand what we need to cherish. I understand what matters. I understand that the gift of life, and of family and friends, and of feeling still a part of the world, is beyond exceptional. And the fact that I have breath in me tells me there is so much still to be grateful for. Through this calm assurance that life can be wonderful again, I will always be sensitive to the fragility and unpredictability of the sorrow that we all must breathe.

I try my best to live for today and to be grateful for this difficult world. Through this reluctant path of survival, I can see that there are still so many things worth living and hoping for. While the loss of my husband will always be a part of my sorrows, the journey I am on is renewed, and I am thankful for the experiences I still have ahead, the memories that will never leave me, and the dreams I continue to dream. Basically, life most certainly does go on. Even in those darkest moments, there is always light somewhere.

I will leave you with an excerpt from Max Ehrmann's "Desiderata,"
written in 1927.

> And whether or not is clear to you, no doubt the uni-
> verse is unfolding as it should. Therefore, be at peace
> with God, whatever you conceive Him to be. And what-
> ever your labors and aspirations, in the noisy confusion
> of life, keep peace in your soul. With all its sham, and
> drudgery and broken dreams, it is still a beautiful world.
> Be cheerful. Strive to be happy.

PART TWO

THE PAIN THROUGH POETRY

I wrote the following poems during my experience with cancer and even beyond. They are poems that are unedited, raw, written in real time, and offered in no particular order. They all reflect the same thing, just written at different moments in the time of this sorrow. I do not apologize for its infantile format, or its incorrect pentameter, for each word is a unique beating of my heart. Each word reflects my sorrow, my disbelief, and my reality at a time when I could not see beyond the cancer.

This is my written journey through the unbearable pain and heartache of losing my husband. All the poems were written for him, except "I Can't Do This," which was written after finding out my beloved brother-in-law had terminal cancer.

Devastations

The symptoms, the visit, the diagnosis, the consultations;
The treatment, the trial, the consternations;
The living, the existing, the hoping and the realizations;
The ups, the downs, the failings and the postulations;
The sickness, the disease, and the hospitalizations;
The hospice, the medicines, the sorrow and the tribulations;
The death, the loss, the shock and the desperations;
The exhaustion, the exasperation, and the finalization;
The Grief Group and the discussions and the tears and the memories;
The pathos of love lost, and dreams shattered—
Such devastations.

Invisible

Let me disappear in the world today, for a moment, for a time, for a while.
Let me not be the focus, the center, or the wings that flight depends on.
Let me shine softly rather than exude a brilliance that blinds.
Let me walk gently rather than leave footprints wherever I go.
I want to feel the void; I want to feel the nothingness that being invisible
    may bring—
Not to shut away the world, but to take the attention somewhere else,
    to quietly *be*.
Let me take my breaths sweetly; let my heart beat only for the one I
    wish to hear it.
Let my words sink into your heart, even though you are not near.
Let my moments dance again, but may they tiptoe through life and
    not run.
Let my fingertips touch your hand but brush you with my love and not
    take hold.
I want to know you again, to understand you, to be in and a part
    of you—
Not to weaken you but to quietly strengthen you and build you up.
Let my sorrows fade into the ocean and tremble as the thunder.
Let what was, what is, and what may be only sit upon the branch of life.
Let me not wonder, or ponder, or question; just let me be.
Let love wash over me again and again, loving before and during and after.
I want to be invisible and let fate skip over my life, pass me by as if I
    were not here,
Not to dismiss my being, but to embrace the knowledge that silence
    can heal.

My Broken Heart

Broken hearts, broken dreams:
Kisses stolen in the night when the touch of
a young man makes you flutter,
Young love with so much hope, tender glances promised the world.

Broken hearts, broken dreams:
I had my heart shattered and put the pieces back together again,
Thinking all was lost;
Then you came into my life, and I never
knew a better love, a better man.

Broken hearts, broken dreams:
Everyone has at least one.
Your love embraced me, protected me, held me close to you;
I was swallowed up by your kindness, your wisdom, and your goals.

Broken hearts, broken dreams:
We loved; oh, how we loved, how we loved each other!
We grew together and created our family, our world, our heaven.

Broken hearts, broken dreams:
Cancer came and took you away like a silent thief in the night.
I couldn't hold you here in this existence, though how I tried!
I never knew what a broken heart really was until you broke mine;
I never knew what broken dreams looked like until you left this world.

Broken hearts, broken dreams …

Quiet Noise

All I can hear is the pain of my heart, pulsating with sorrow, beating to
    loneliness.
The walls that surround me hold blank stares; nothing moves.
The streets and the business of life seem vacant, going nowhere.
There is silence that is deafening …
I listen for your voice, for your footsteps, for evidence that you are here.
I am broken by the silence, engulfed by the emptiness, shattered by the
    quiet noise.
I walk through darkness, though the sun beats heavily on me.
There is nothing inside me, though blood flows strongly through my
    veins.
I breathe, I breathe … but is this my life? What now? What next? What
    is this all about?
Let me hear you once again, let me know you are still here, somewhere,
    though you are not with me.
The winds of broken dreams suffocate me like a hurricane of storms;
I am drowning in heartache, losing this battle of love lost.
Bonds cannot be broken with the world we had,
but I am broken still without you, my darling—
Strangled slowly by the quiet noise, by the constant painful cry of my
    broken heart.

The Journey

I see death as a journey. You were put on this vessel, and it is slowly
    taking you away
from me, from all that we were.
Silently you drift away, drift toward this unknown shore. I am here still,
    on the ground
that we called home, on the land that was our life, on the roads that we
    traveled on ...
but there you go. Off and away from me.
Slowly you drift. Quietly you are taken away like a prisoner, held captive.
    I watch as you
reach this foreign horizon and suddenly I cannot see you anymore. You
    are gone from me, my love. You are gone.

Little Things

I still call you, with your cell number clearly in my head.
I still email you, text you, call for you.
I still wait to hear your footsteps as you come home from work
or hear your voice call out my name.
I still see you smiling back at me, keeping me
where I should be, always with you.
I still long for life to be different, for the years to reverse,
for us to be young and new again.
I still wait for my heart to stop bleeding, for my tears to stop flowing,
for you to come home to me.
I long for you to be here, just breathing and being, as we always did,
being us, being in love, being free from cancer.
The little things that once were so sublime, so
unimportant in the everyday moments,
are now what matters most.
Your car still is parked in our driveway, and
your clothes still are hanging, waiting
for you to put them on.
I'll make you tea: two sugars or one, cream or milk?
We can watch our favorite shows together, just you and me.
The seasons somehow have lost their beauty,
though they still stumble on,
as I have lost my glow, and I too stumble on,
I lack all ability to move through this; life is profoundly changed.
Sorrow is everywhere, you are gone, I cannot believe it to be true.

Three little things I want to say to you, to tell you once again,
if I didn't tell you enough:
Love continues, despite what has been taken away;
we are still together, even though you
are not here; being broken and torn does not mean the end of us.

Parched Throat

I brought you popsicles to soothe your parched throat,
Perhaps to give you something to enjoy, something to delight.
I changed the sheets and put a warm, soft blanket on the bed,
Perhaps to keep you warmer during those long nights.
I washed your clothes and kept your razor charged,
Perhaps to give you a purpose for each day.
I found you books of substance and writing tools
So we could have our talks in our special way.
They are all reminders now that you don't need them anymore.

Walking Dead

I am walking dead. Like you, I cannot see,
though my eyes are searching.
Like you, I cannot hear, though my ears are opened.
Like you, I cannot think, though my head is clear.

I am walking dead. Like you, I cannot see
the sun, though it is shining.
Like you, I cannot feel the wind, though it is surely blowing.
Like you, I cannot feel the ground beneath
my feet, though I am standing.

I am walking dead. Stumbling. Slipping.
Crawling. Crying. Broken. Bruised.
Unlike you, I am still here, but you are gone.
I am walking dead.

The Strength of Sorrow

I long for you every day with every breath I take. I long for your
footsteps across the floor, your voice filling the space.
I long for your laughter that makes me smile inside,
And I long for your words that comfort me.
I cry from every pore, from every pore of my body.
I cry with a strength of sorrow that is beyond that of any army.
I cry with such power that I feel I will cease to exist, as you did,
And I cry because I cannot bear such pain.
My tears, my pain, my broken heart are now my constant companions.
I do not know life anymore without the existence of sorrow.
You are not with me, and I have lost my essence; you were my breath.
My tears flow and flow … my heart continues to break every day.
I simply do not know how to do this.

The Cage

Accepting this reality, accepting that you are gone from me,
accepting that I can no longer on this earth hear your voice,
hold your hand, or feel your body next to mine
is not going to be easy.

I am forced into the corner of this cage that is my life,
scared, fighting, kicking, screaming that this cannot be.
I bang against the metal barriers that hold me captive,
forcing me to swallow this poison of your death.

I cannot go gently into this reality. I am fighting, fighting,
fighting for you, fighting with every fiber of my being …
but no matter how I fight, you are still not here.
I can't fight you back to life.

So I succumb to the horror of this cage, locked inside, trapped,
hopeless and helpless. I crawl into the corner as if I could disappear,
but I am still visible and being watched
with eyes eager to see what I will do next.

But honestly, what can I do?

Fight

A golden tease of color, just over the mountainside, tempts me to see
the beauty before me.
The sunshine is beaming in her glory high over
my head, embraced by a sky so softly blue.
The tender air is chasing me, surrounding me with gentle caresses,
and the gilded trees stand tall and strong
and plentiful before my eyes. I see
the rhythmic dance of the ocean and hear the
waves singing with a calm repose.
A peaceful waterfall rolls down the hill, whispering my name.
All around me is picturesque and magical, and yet
without you, I have to fight to open my eyes
to see such things. I have to fight
to recognize the beauty before me. I have to
fight to understand that this is our life.
I am here without you, and you are without the
glorious mountainsides and sunshine
and sweet air. You are without the trees and
the oceans and the waterfalls.

We tried to fight this disease, didn't we?
I hate being brave, but I'm told I must be.
I hate the sunshine when I prefer the night.
I hate pretending that I can walk upright
when I'm so exhausted from this fight.
I hate the tears that I must hide.
I hate the words that hurt my pride.
I hate the worry, the constant fear

when I all I know is you're not here.
I hate that fate took hold of us;
I hate that life has broken us.
I hate that I must do this alone
when all I want is for you to come home.
I love that you and I found truth.
I even love that the road wasn't always smooth.
I love you still, my darling dear;
I just hate that you're not here.

I Can't Do This

For Bill

I can't hear what you're saying. Did you say "cancer"?
I can't understand what you're saying. Did you say "cancer"?
I can't believe what you're saying. Did you say "cancer"?

I can't hear what you're saying. Did you say "chemo"?
I can't understand what you're saying. Did you say that it has *spread*?
I can't believe what you're saying. Did you say "no hope"?

I stop listening, I stop processing, and I
stop trying to absorb all of this.
I'm trying to ask why, trying to believe in
miracles, trying to hope for a cure.

I can't hear what you're saying. Did you say "cancer"?
I can't believe what you're saying. Did you say "no hope"?

Spilled Coffee

My life is like spilled coffee, seeping into every crevice possible—falling, dripping, spilled, and wasted.

I am fluid and not contained, moving through sorrow, hot, cold, wandering, and lost.

There is no way to put life in reverse, to pick up the terrible spill of death and put life back neatly in its cup.

I can no longer drink of the joy and happiness that being with you gave me; there is no more to taste in life, it seems.

My world is like spilled coffee: I can still smell the laughter and the memories, but I see it all slipping away, drip by drip.

I'm trying to clean up this mess, but it will never be the same.

A Good Day

Didn't cry all day but cried a bit
got out of bed though fighting it

made it to work and errands too
tried not to think too much of you

broke down just once when I thought too deep
of moments lost, when we were free

too much weight to carry on
hard to stand now that you are gone

a good day I guess when the day was done
I laughed a bit even had some fun

but never so far from sorrow's grip
walking the heartbreak cliff I sometimes slip

missing you but smiling still
because life goes on despite my will

the sun provokes with its brilliant test
the evening comes and the darkness rests

a true good day will not be had
but another day is what I have

without you I am not alive
but a good day tells me I must survive

the dullness of a constant pain
asking, *Will I see you again?*

The Lost Glove

Somewhere along the way, I lost my glove. I lost
something that broke the pair. I lost
the match, the other one, the right hand to the left hand.
I lost my glove.
I loved this glove, wore it proudly; it kept me warm and cozy. But what
do I do now? I will never find the match to the
glove that was left behind. I will never
complete this pair, which will never be whole again.
The glove that is still here is a body without a
soul, lying lifeless on the shelf, waiting
for its mate to be found. But day by day, night
by night, the distance grows farther
from the hope that it will return.
I am cold; the glove is gone.

Nearby

Do you wake with me, dear, as I stumble from our bed,
Looking to a day without you ahead?
Do you drink my morning cup of tea with me
And sit with me as things used to be?
Do you walk with me as I find my way around
And hold me up when I feel I will fall down?
Do you whisper sweet nothings as I lay my head to sleep
With promises that you may never keep?
You must be here somewhere, my love, standing by,
Holding me close when you see me cry.
You see me faint, and my heart is weak
Just wanting you when I go to sleep.
You have to be somewhere within these walls,
Listening to me when I call.
You are my life, my love, my hope; keep me near.
Tell me it will be okay, and calm my fears.

Secrets

Somewhere in the midst of this darkness, I try to find the light that will take me out of this pain.

I look for hope in the stars, a promise in the gardens, or a song from the sweet birds as they sing to me.

Beneath the exterior that I have neatened up, I am but a broken mess that no one knows.

I keep you close, I say your name, I hold your hand and pretend that you will walk through that door.

When I don't know what to do or how to act, I listen to your voice helping me through as you would always do.

When my withered heart and lingering sorrow break my back and I cannot hold this pain anymore, I call your name and listen for your heartbeat. Perhaps around the corner, perhaps somewhere, you are waiting for me.

Secretly I have not left the world that we created, and I will not do so soon. My darling, you must know that I have locked my memories in a private box so as not to lose you twice.

What I cannot bear, what I cannot believe, what I cannot understand, is that you are not here with me. Here in this world. Our world.

Just tell me a soft secret of life that continues, of love that will endure, of a time when we will be together again.

Where Did You Go

Where did you go when you slipped away that night? Quietly into an
   invisible darkness that I couldn't see.
Where did you go when you reached for me with a weakened grasp and
   silently left me?
Where did you go when you lay on that bed, without a word, just slip-
   ping silently away?
Where did you go, my darling? I ask this every day.
If only I knew of this new place of yours that has taken you from me,
taken you to a place that I truly cannot see—
Are you there somewhere in these rooms of ours, where once you walked
   with ease?
Are you whispering things to me each day that I cannot foresee?
Are you trying to hold me tight? Do you want to hold my hand?
Oh, tell me, darling, dear of mine, for I do not understand.
You left me here; you would never go, but death took you away,
And I cry myself to sleep each night after I've faced the day.
Without you the sun should fall, the moon should disappear;
The stars should burn out quickly because you're not here.
Where did you go when you slipped away that night? Quietly into an
   invisible darkness that I could not see.
Please, dear God, awaken me, and put my heart together again, for this
   simply cannot be.

Commotion

All this commotion around us, yet you are still.
The water rises, the clouds darken, and the
winds cry out, yet you are still.
All this turmoil finds us, yet you are still.
The noise deafens, the light blinds, and the words
fall on empty hopes, yet you are still.
All this darkness swallows us up, yet you are still.
The night closes in, the morning cries out,
the noon weeps, yet you are still.
All this pain engulfs us, yet you are still.
The heart beats, but barely; tears flow constantly,
sorrow abides, yet you are still.
Let me see movement again, let me see you
breathe life again, don't be still.
Let the commotion and the turmoil and the
darkness and the pain be still,
but let it not be that you are still.

If Only ...

I woke up this morning and you were there next to me. We talked about
our day ahead.
You had a lot of meetings; I had my social groups and lunch meetings.
I texted you at noon to see what you wanted for dinner and to check in
on your day. You were fine, thought about ordering pizza and renting
a movie. Perfect.
I did my errands, called the kids, walked the dogs, and did the laundry. You called my name when you got home, and we kissed hello.
Exchanged a few things about our day and went on about our own
things still needing to be done.
You napped before pizza. We found a great movie and cuddled up to
watch it. The dogs cuddled with us. A perfect night together.
I cleaned up the dishes, said I was going to bed early, and you did some
more work in your office before going to bed. I heard you walking
around the house. I think you made tea, spoke to someone on the
phone.
Then I heard you walk up the stairs to come to bed.
I love you, I said. Have a good sleep. You cuddled next to me, and we
fell into a gentle sleep. So wonderfully normal.
And still you are gone, and each day I live in a prison of footsteps heard
but unheard, pizza and movies, kisses goodnight that are mine
alone—
Simply no more of you.

It Was Your Liver

Your hair, though graying, was still soft and silky,
Your eyes bright with life and hope.
Your skin was taut and strong and white,
And your hands could still hold me close.
Your legs carried you through the day with persistence,
And your feet walked though fear and sorrow with such force.
Your heart beat every day for another moment, another memory,
And your blood flowed through your veins with continued intensity.
Your mind—your brilliant, thoughtful, creative
mind—still wanted to learn and to teach.
Your thoughts traveled to hope and back, only staying in the moment.
It was your liver that could not sustain your beautiful body and soul.
It was your liver that took your life.

Walk through the Door

Walk through the door, please—
Come home after work as you used to do.
Make yourself a cup of tea and put on the baseball game.
Tell me of your day.

Walk through the door, please—
Kiss me hello, and let us talk.
Fill the spaces of our home once again with your voice.

Walk through the door, please,
For I cannot bear to think that you will never
walk through that door again.

Submission

Cornered, I cry, I cringe, I crumble.
Silenced, I scream, I search, I stumble.
Broken, I am bewildered. I beg, I become empty.
How can I submit to this fate?

Perhaps like a tender kitten that softly tiptoes into the room,
gently leaving a trace of what was.
Or maybe like the thunderous storms that pass over the skies,
falling rain that pounds on the standing ground.
We are forced either way to accept this, you and I.
We are not offered a choice. I say, "Please, no!" I say, "I love you,"
and though you are somewhere, I can't hear what you are saying.
In this submission you have been silenced, and I feel that my
very heartbeat has been silenced too.
There is loneliness, a vast empty void that
just *is*, and the devastating pain
of knowing that fate has found us, descended upon us, and taken you.
We could not fight this. We could not close
the door to the horror of it all.
The world looks different, the sunshine feels different,
and I cannot find the balance of life anymore. I just *am*.
We were something, weren't we? Something magical,
wonderful and warm, and oh so real.

How can I submit to this fate?
Emptied, I ache; I ache until I cannot bear this pain.
The sorrow hardens around me into nothingness.
I kneel in prayer again and again.

Submitting myself, I accept this devastation; and so,
Fate,
do not ask this of me.
I will fight you until my own breath becomes air;
I will not allow you to think this is okay.
Unlike the tenderness of a kitten nor the strength of a storm,
I will not give in to this.

I Miss Us

I miss us. I miss a normal day, filled with normal life before us.
I don't ask any more than that. I miss us.
I miss you. I miss you and me together. I miss our family being whole.
I miss what we were and what we were to be in the coming years.
I miss our dreams and plans and hopes.
I miss the future that we thought we had.
I miss what would have been now. I miss the days that we have lost.
I miss movie times, and I miss Saturday lunches.
I miss you barbecuing, and I miss you golfing.
I miss holding your hand, looking into your beautiful eyes.
I miss your brilliance and your innocence. I miss you so much.
I miss your voice, your footsteps. I miss
knowing that you are breathing.
I miss just being. Just living. Just existing
with the expectation that we would.
I miss happiness and joy and the comfort of a peaceful day.
I miss us. I miss my best friend. I miss feeling that life was okay.
I now know pain too well; I understand the depths of sorrow
and the vast pangs of loneliness. I understand hopelessness and fear.
I am changed. We are changed. It is a long
journey without you, a path I never imagined.
I miss believing that we are rewarded for
goodness, that there is a balance to fate.
I miss the hope that blessings abound. I miss miracles.
I miss believing that you would be okay. Believing in the treatment.
I miss believing in a cure.
I miss you. Oh how I miss you, my love.

Fade Away

Letting go, sifting through the years,
watching everything fade away …
Who am I anymore? Where do I belong? Nothing is as it should be.
Every step I take I see a memory, I hear a voice, laughter, tears, our life.
Through the silence and brutality of my
existence, I ponder on what was.
It is all invisible now, painfully gone, tragically over.
The years have taken us far from what we used to have,
what we guarded with our love, the house that we found ourselves
to absorb into our hearts, the land that carried us and held us stable,
the gardens that grow and protect and beautify. How do I let go?
I step out alone. No one to hold my hand.
No one to tell me it will be okay.
It's not okay. Everything has changed. My heart
weeps and is torn with each memory.
How can I let go of all that was, of all that
we had, of all that should be?
I am weary, broken and stabbed with the pain of missing you.
Where is joy? Where is God? Where is the answer?
Where are you? Where? Don't fade away; stay, memories, stay.

Home

There is no place like home, where comfort abides, and warmth ensues, where memories softly drift through the rooms.

There is no place like home where the voices linger, where the babies cry gently, tender words are whispered, and laughter rings. Even tears and angry voices dance about.

But when you are gone, there is no home, no place to find comfort. The warmth melts away, and we are frozen into place at the moment our home changed.

You once said that I was your home, that wherever we were was home, and so without you, I cannot be home.

I exist waiting for the moment when we are united, longing for the arms of stability to embrace me, for memories to start again, for the rooms to fill with life and excitement, and to glow with happiness.

You are my home; you are my life. Without you, I am as empty and vast and lonely as could possibly be.

Reckless

I am responsible yet reckless.
I am strong but broken.
I am surrounded but lonely.
I am alive but dead.
I am driven but stagnant.
I am here but not here.
You are there but not here.
I am crying always.

I Wish

I wish that you could have forgotten that today is my birthday. And I wish that you would have bought me roses with a card at the last minute.

I wish that I could ask you to roll over so that I could have more space in bed, and I wish that you could tell me that I was taking all the blankets.

I wish that I could ask you why you forgot to take out the trash, and then I wish that I could ask if you remembered to buy milk.

I wish that we could argue again or get mad at each other over a silly thing, and then I wish that we could make up and think all was well.

I wish that I could ask you if you would pick up your laundry from the floor, or tell you that you snored too loud. I wish that all of these daily insignificant things could just be.

The "nothing special" and the "nothing magical" moments turn out to be the most treasured in our lifetime, and so most of all, I wish that we had many more of these "nothing special" and "nothing magical" moments together.

I wish with all my heart that cancer did not take you, and I wish that they had found a cure instead. I wish most of all that you were here. That is all.

Holding On

I tried to hold on to you. I tried to cling and grab and reach and stick to you in every way. I tried to hold on with all my heart.

You were my existence, you were my breath, you were my reason. Letting go meant accepting that you were slipping away. Letting go was devastating. It broke me. It destroyed me. It crushed my very soul.

I held on to you for a long time after you left; you were planted in my heart. I listened for you. I waited for you. I wanted to believe that you would come back, but you didn't. You simply couldn't.

Our children cling now to me. They hold me. They reach for me. They stick to me in every way. And so really, we hold on to you still.

Take the Miracle

Grasping, gasping, reaching for anything;
Waiting, wishing, hoping for the impossible;

Crying, clinging, praying *Let it be him*;
Kneeling, needing, knowing that it may not—

Grief becomes selfish. We think it should be us.
The miracle should be ours.

Why save the children? Why save the young soldiers
Who miss their homes?

Why save the mothers or the puppies
Who make us smile?

Why save the innocent or the deprived
Who never knew peace?

I'll take the miracle, I say, just this once
Over anyone else.

Let him live.

ABOUT THE AUTHOR

Carole Ann Baer, a distinguished figure in the ballroom dance world, has achieved notable success as a performer and educator. She studied special education and psychology at Brigham Young University where she also danced with the Brigham Young University Ballroom Dance Team and currently teaches dance at Brandeis University. She has a passion for cultural, community and service-oriented programs and currently is the Commissioner and founder of the Sudbury Little League Challenger Division as well as one of the founding members of HOPEsudbury. Baer lives in Stow, Massachusetts.

David Baer, Lee Baer, Emily Baer and Carole-Ann
Baer, along with their dogs Paisley and Daisy.

Photo courtesy of Paige Gilbert-Goldfarb/www.photosbypaige.com

Memorial bench located along the shore path in Bar Harbor, Maine

Printed in the United States
by Baker & Taylor Publisher Services